INDIGENOUS BIOGRAPHIES

Red Cloud

Military Leader

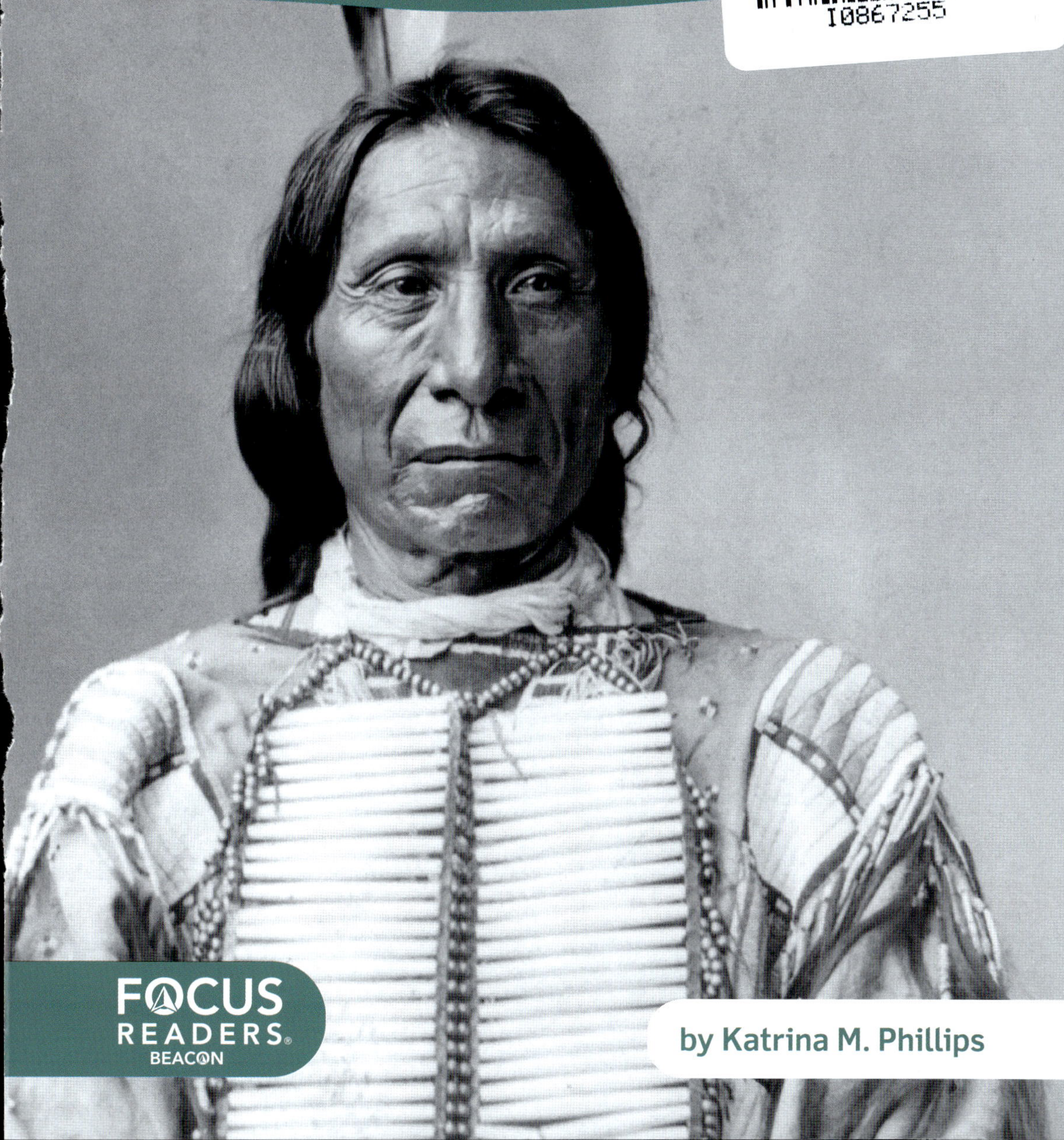

FOCUS READERS BEACON

by Katrina M. Phillips

www.focusreaders.com

Focus Readers is distributed by North Star Editions:
sales@northstareditions.com | 888-417-0195

Produced for Focus Readers by Red Line Editorial.

Photographs ©: Library of Congress, cover, 1, 11, 19; William Henry Jackson/National Archives, 4; National Portrait Gallery/Smithsonian Institution, 6, 29; Shutterstock Images, 8, 22; Historic Images/Alamy, 13; Hannah Hunsinger/Rapid City Journal/AP Images, 15; National Archives, 16, 21, 25; Stephen Groves/AP Images, 27

Library of Congress Cataloging-in-Publication Data
Names: Phillips, Katrina M., author
Title: Red Cloud: military leader / by Katrina M. Phillips.
Description: Mendota Heights, MN: Focus Readers, [2026] | Series: Indigenous biographies | Includes bibliographical references and index. | Audience: Grades 2-3
Identifiers: LCCN 2025012041 (print) | LCCN 2025012042 (ebook) | ISBN 9798889985044 hardcover | ISBN 9798889986584 paperback | ISBN 9798889985679 ebook pdf | ISBN 9798889985365 hosted ebook
Subjects: LCSH: Red Cloud, 1822-1909 | Lakota Indians--Biography--Juvenile literature | Red Cloud's War, 1866-1867--Juvenile literature | Lakota Indians--History--19th century--Juvenile literature | LCGFT: Biographies | Literature.
Classification: LCC E99.T34 P46 2026 (print) | LCC E99.T34 (ebook) | DDC 978.004/9752440092 [B]--dc23/eng/20250416
LC record available at https://lccn.loc.gov/2025012041
LC ebook record available at https://lccn.loc.gov/2025012042

Printed in the United States of America
Mankato, MN
012026

About the Author

Dr. Katrina M. Phillips (Red Cliff Ojibwe) is a writer, researcher, and history professor. She's written several children's books about Native histories and cultures, including *Indigenous Peoples' Day* and *I Am on Indigenous Land*. She and her husband live in Minnesota with their two sons and their goofy dog.

Table of Contents

CHAPTER 1

Victory in the West

In 1863, the **Bozeman Trail** opened. It led west to gold-mining areas. But the trail ran through Native lands. Thousands of miners and settlers trespassed on these lands.

In the 1800s, hundreds of thousands of non-Native people moved west to look for gold.

Red Cloud is one of the most respected leaders in Lakota history.

Native nations fought back. Oglala leader Red Cloud played a major role. Red Cloud helped bring Lakota, Arapaho, and Cheyenne people together. He also led several battles against the US Army.

This became known as Red Cloud's War (1866–1868). After two years, the government wanted the fighting to end. US leaders asked for a **treaty**. They agreed to close the Bozeman Trail. It was a victory for leaders such as Red Cloud.

Did You Know?

Red Cloud signed the treaty in 1868. It is called the Treaty of Fort Laramie.

CHAPTER 2

A Lakota Life

Red Cloud was born in 1822. His father's name was Lone Man. His mother's name was Walks As She Thinks. Lone Man died when Red Cloud was young. His mother took her children to live with her people.

Red Cloud grew up learning to hunt bison on the Great Plains.

Red Cloud was raised in the **traditional** Oglala way. Oglala boys such as Red Cloud learned to hunt. They learned to ride ponies and horses. They learned to protect their people.

But the Lakota world was changing quickly. Americans kept moving west. They wanted land.

Did You Know?

The Lakota people are made up of seven bands. The Oglala are one of them.

Spotted Tail was a leader of the Lakota's Sicangu band. In the 1850s, he fiercely opposed settlers taking Lakota land.

They wanted precious resources such as gold and silver. Americans wanted to build railroads, too.

They thought Native nations stood in their way.

Leaders such as Red Cloud did not want to give up their lands. They did not want to give up their ways of life. Wars and battles broke out across the Great Plains. Red Cloud fought in many of these battles. His bravery in battle earned him respect. He became known as a great warrior.

The Lakota were not the only ones who fought back. Many Native

Red Cloud worked with Northern Cheyenne leaders Little Wolf (left) and Dull Knife (right).

nations across the West refused to move to **reservations**. They refused to sign treaties with the US government.

TOPIC SPOTLIGHT

Lakota Values

Lakota people live by seven values. Values are beliefs that help guide actions. They show what is important to people. The seven values include generosity, respect, and wisdom. Another value is kinship. This is someone's extended family. The fifth value is prayer. Many Lakota people speak to the Creator. The sixth value is compassion. This means caring for others. The seventh is fortitude. This means facing challenges with courage and strength. Red Cloud learned these values from his people. These values are still important for many Lakota people today.

Lakota values are often passed down generation to generation.

THE BOZEMAN TRAIL

CHAPTER 3

Red Cloud's War

Miners and settlers kept building trails through Native lands. The Bozeman Trail was only one of these trails. The trail was the easiest way to travel to what is now Montana.

People often took wagon trains along the Bozeman Trail.

The US government also kept building forts. Fort Laramie was at the start of the Bozeman Trail. This fort stood in what is now Wyoming.

Miners on the trail killed the bison. Settlers' cattle ate too much grass. These changes made it hard for Lakota people to find food.

Did You Know?

Bison were one of the most important resources for Native nations on the Great Plains.

Red Cloud's victories in battle helped force the US government to ask for a treaty.

This led to Red Cloud's War. Native nations attacked wagon trains. The US Army sent soldiers for protection. But after two years, the US Army still hadn't stopped the attacks. So, US officials asked for a treaty.

Some Native leaders signed the treaty in the spring of 1868. But Red Cloud did not trust the US leaders. They did not always keep their promises to Native people. Red Cloud waited until the forts came down. He waited until the Bozeman Trail was closed. Red Cloud finally signed the treaty in November.

Lakota leaders agreed to some things they hadn't wanted. For example, Red Cloud and others

US and Native leaders gather for the signing of the Treaty of Fort Laramie in 1868.

agreed to move to a reservation. However, the treaty promised the Lakota could always live there. The Lakota could keep their sacred **Black Hills**.

CHAPTER 4

Red Cloud's Legacy

The United States soon broke its promises. Americans found gold in the Black Hills in 1874. Thousands of miners and settlers moved onto Lakota lands. They ignored the Treaty of Fort Laramie.

As of 2025, the United States hadn't returned the Black Hills to the Lakota.

The US government forced the Lakota to give up the Black Hills.

The Lakota did not want to give up the Black Hills. Red Cloud and others spoke out against the government. But government officials did not change their minds. They would not uphold the treaty. This led to another war.

Red Cloud did not fight in the war. He had signed the treaty in 1868. He had promised to follow the terms of the treaty. But he

Red Cloud (center, seated) visits Washington, DC, with a group of Oglala leaders in the 1870s.

spent the rest of his life fighting for Native rights. He took many trips to Washington, DC. He criticized federal **policies**. He did not want to see Native children sent to **boarding schools**.

Red Cloud's life ended quietly. He died in 1909 in South Dakota. Red Cloud was nearly 90 years old. His life had been marked by many changes. He had helped lead the Lakota in times of war and peace. He had tried to preserve Lakota ways of life.

Did You Know?

Red Cloud's **descendants** still serve as traditional leaders for the Lakota people.

Henry Red Cloud is the great-great-grandson of Red Cloud. He works on training Native people on green energy such as solar power.

Focus Questions

Write your answers on a separate piece of paper.

1. Write a letter to a friend describing what you learned about treaties.
2. Would you have sided with Red Cloud? Why or why not?
3. What is the name of the treaty Red Cloud signed?
   - **A.** Treaty of the Black Hills
   - **B.** Treaty of Fort Laramie
   - **C.** Treaty of the Bozeman Trail
4. Why did Red Cloud not take part in the Great Sioux War?
   - **A.** He was too old, and he was no longer able to walk.
   - **B.** He didn't believe the war was worth fighting.
   - **C.** He had signed a treaty agreeing not to fight.

5. What does **trespassed** mean in this book?

*However, the trail ran through Native lands. Thousands of miners and settlers **trespassed** on these lands.*

A. entered another's land without permission

B. returned to one's original home

C. discovered a new resource

6. What does **ignored** mean in this book?

*Thousands of miners and settlers moved onto Lakota lands. They **ignored** the Treaty of Fort Laramie.*

A. paid attention to

B. put into place

C. did not pay attention to

Answer key on page 32.

Glossary

Black Hills
A mountain range in the Great Plains. Lakota people consider it the most sacred place in the world.

boarding schools
Places where Native children were forced to learn English and forget their cultures.

Bozeman Trail
A trail that ran through part of the American West. It was named after John Bozeman, one of the men who made the route.

descendants
People who come from a certain family, ancestor, or group of people.

policies
Laws and practices that lay out the US government's relationship with Native nations.

reservations
Land set aside by the US government for Native nations.

traditional
Following a group's common practices.

treaty
An official agreement that is made between two or more countries or groups.

To Learn More

BOOKS

Beason, Jimmy. *Native Americans in History: A History Book for Kids.* Rockridge Press, 2021.

Lombardo, Jennifer. *Red Cloud.* Cavendish Square Publishing, 2025.

Sorell, Traci. *We Are Still Here! Native American Truths Everyone Should Know.* Charlesbridge Publishing, 2021.

NOTE TO EDUCATORS

Visit **www.focusreaders.com** to find links and resources related to this title.

Index

Answer Key: 1. Answers will vary; 2. Answers will vary; 3. B; 4. C; 5. A; 6. C